# PLANT BASED COOKBOOK FOR BEGINNERS

Easy and Healthy
Plant Based Recipes for
Healthy Eating

JASON YOTHERS

# contents

# contents

## SOUPS AND SALADS  71

# contents

# INTRODUCTION

# WHAT IS PLANT-BASED DIET?

As the name suggests, a plant-based diet includes food items that majorly come from plants. Such a diet revolves around vegetables, fruits, seeds, nuts, beans, whole grains, and legumes as well.

Heart disease and cancer are two of the biggest health issues of humankind. According to many studies, whole plant-based foods provide protection to your body from life-threatening diseases.

Plant-based diet shifts you away from animal products, artificial foods, processed products, added flavors, and other harmful components. As a result, your body receives safe nutrition without facing a risk of deadly diseases.

# BENEFITS OF PLANT-BASED DIET

After shifting your diet toward 100% plants, you can attain a great overall health along with other protective advantages. There are various protein options available in the plant-based diet as well. So, you don't have to worry about the shortage of protein in your body.

In fact, there are many professional athletes and celebrities who follow plant-based eating habits.

Going plant-based is easy, as you can find all products anywhere near your place. At the same time, you save a lot of money, as plant-based food products don't cost as much as the animal-based products.

With plant-based diet, you can experience all the following benefits:

## 1. CONTROLLED BLOOD PRESSURE

The immediate and most visible early benefit of this diet is the reduction in blood pressure. People struggle with high levels of blood pressure due to oily, processed animal-based food items. Removing that allows your body to obtain rich potassium content from safer sources.

With potassium obtained from plant-based foods, blood pressure of your body gets controlled. The balanced blood pressure tends to resolve the problems of anxiety and stress.

There are plenty of plant resources to obtain potassium. Such resources include whole grains, nuts, legumes, seeds, nuts, vegetables, and fruits. Along with potassium, all the given resources also provide a high content of vitamin B6, which also improves the balance of blood sugar in your body.

## 2. REDUCTION IN CHOLESTEROL

One of the biggest benefits plant-based diet offers is the reduction in cholesterol level.

Almost every food item from plants contains no or very little cholesterol. Lower cholesterol level in your body saves from heart diseases.

But that lower cholesterol won't be possible if you keep having animal products such as eggs, meat or fish. They all contain a high amount of cholesterol, which ruins the performance capacity of your heart.

## 3. BALANCED BLOOD SUGAR LEVELS

The most effective way to balance your blood sugar level is including more fiber in your diet. Fibers help in convenient absorption of the excess sugar running in your blood stream.

With sugars absorbed, you don't feel too hungry, which helps your mind and body altogether. Balanced blood sugar keeps your body in optimum health conditions and allows your mind to feel stress-free.

A plant-based diet is a great way to ensure consistent availability of fiber in your diet. At the same time, you don't eat high-sugar content, which assists in controlling the blood sugar levels.

## 4. REDUCED RISK OF CANCER

Whole foods, low-fat content, and high fiber, all these traits of plant-based foods improve your ability to stay away from cancer. Of course, you have to follow the diet with discipline and also stay away from bad habits of alcohol and smoking.

There are many animal foods that boost the risk of cancer. Breast cancer and colon cancer are two common kinds that have been related to animal-based food items.

Plant-based diet protects you from the risks of animal foods and allows you to live a cancer-free life.

## 5. WEIGHT LOSS

If your goal is to lose weight without compromising the nutritional quality of your diet, this eating habit is effective. The guidelines and food options of this diet keep you away from processed sugars and high-fat content.

With that, you can lose weight without compromising your strength or energy. You eat clean and healthy food choices and intake fiber, minerals, and vitamins.

Along with all that, plant-based diet is also known to make your digestion better. The problem of constipation reduces. Also, the problem of inflammation reduces as well.

All in all, a plant-based diet is an effective way of eating to live a long life without struggling with critical diseases. At the same time, you can eat well and feel the improved strength in your body.

# WHAT TO EAT AND WHAT TO AVOID

Eating restrictions are pretty easy to understand in this diet.

There is a wide range of whole plant-based products allowed in the diet.

In this way, you will be receiving a great variety to try new dishes.

FRUITS: All kinds of whole fruits are allowed in this diet. You just have to have fruits in their organic form. Don't use fruit juices or dried fruits and other refined options.

VEGETABLES WITH NO STARCH: All vegetables are allowed in the diet such as leafy greens, zucchini, broccoli, tomatoes, eggplant, and others.

VEGETABLES WITH STARCH: Vegetables with starch content are also accepted in this diet. So, you can utilize potatoes, legumes, sweet potatoes, beans, corn, peas, plantains, squash, and others.

# WHAT TO EAT IN A PLANT-BASED DIET

WHOLE GRAINS: All whole grains with 100% purity are allowed in this diet. You can utilize brown rice, whole wheat, oats, and other whole grain choices in your plant-based diet.

BEVERAGES: In the category of beverages, you can only use plant-based milk without any sweetness. Also, water, tea, coffee, and green tea are allowed options in this diet.

SPICES: All kinds of spices are accepted in the plant-based diet.

SOURCES OF OMEGA-3: All safe sources of omega-3 are promoted during the plant-based diet. So, you are motivated to include flax seeds, chia seeds, and other resources in your meals.

MEAT: All kinds of meat products such as fish, seafood, poultry, red meat, and even processed meat products are not allowed in a plant-based diet.

EGGS: You can't eat eggs, as it contains high cholesterol content.
DAIRY: All forms of dairy products are not accepted in this diet. You have to avoid milk, yogurt, cream, cheese, buttermilk, and half-and-half.

VEGAN REPLACEMENTS: Vegan replacements of meats and cheese are also not allowed. Such replacements contain high oil content, which is not acceptable in the plant-based diet.

ADDED FAT: You have to say no to all kinds of added fats such as coconut oil, butter, margarine, and all other liquid oils.

# WHAT TO AVOID IN A PLANT-BASED DIET

REFINED FLOURS: Any flour that is not 100% in terms of whole wheat is not accepted. You can't use refined flours in your diet.

ADDED SUGAR: Any food item with added flavoring or sugar is not allowed. Along with that, you have to say no to energy bars, candy bars, cakes, cookies, and all other junk food options.

BEVERAGES: In the category of beverages, you can't have soda or even fruit juices. Even the fruit juices with 100% purity are not allowed. At the same time, you are recommended to stay away from energy drinks, sports drinks, tea drinks, blended coffee, and other harmful beverages that contain flavorings or high-sugar content.

*"Nothing will benefit human health and increase the chances for survival of life on Earth as much as the evolution to a vegetarian diet"*
*- Albert Einstein*

FRESH VEGETABLES AND FRUITS: Look for all varieties of fresh vegetables and fruits you can find. Give priority to leafy greens.

LEGUMES AND BEANS: Dried lentils and beans have multiple varieties available in the market. You can use them all. Just make sure you rinse them before using.

SEEDS AND NUTS: Nuts take the place of liquid oils in your meals. However, you can avoid nuts if you want to lose weight or have a heart condition. Choose seeds of chia and flax to intake high omega-3 content. Similarly, you can purchase other seeds such as sesame, sunflower, and pumpkin.

## SHOPPING LIST

WHOLE GRAIN BREAD AND TORTILLAS: For enchiladas, tacos, burritos, burgers, and other cooking options, you will require whole grain versions of bread and tortillas. Make sure you find 100% pure whole grain buns, tortillas, and bread in the market.

WHOLE GRAINS: The choices of whole grains include quinoa, brown rice, cornmeal, oatmeal, and others. But you need to focus on the wholegrain quality of the choices you pick.

PASTA AND NOODLES OF BROWN RICE: Pasta and noodles of brown rice will help you make some great pasta recipes in different varieties.

CEREALS FOR BREAKFAST: When buying cereals, you have to avoid sweetened ones and the ones that contain added oils. Pick whole grain cereals such as rolled oats, steel cut options of oatmeal, bran flakes, and/or grape nuts.

PLANT-BASED MILK: Nondairy substitutes are required from time to time to gain the smoothness in dishes. You can purchase almond milk, rice milk, soy milk, cashew milk, and other plant-based milk. However, ensure that no milk option contains added flavors or sugars. Also, stay away from products that contain added oils in their milk.

PASTA AND TOMATO SAUCE AND SALSA: Salsa and sauce are a great option when you are cooking pasta. When buying these products, you have to ensure the absence of any animal food content, added oils, and/or sugar content.

## SHOPPING LIST

INSTANT POT: Cooking will get easier with an Instant Pot in your kitchen. You can cook a variety of dishes with just one appliance in your kitchen. Just pick a size that matches your regular cooking quantity.

FOOD PROCESSOR OR BLENDER: A food processor or a blender would be a helpful option when you are cooking vegetable soups or making homemade salsa. So, purchase a high-quality machine to process food items.

*With that, you are now ready to begin your plant-based diet. All you need now is some great recipes, to begin with. So, let's give you a list of breakfast, soups, salads, and main meal recipes.*

# PLANT BASED BREAKFAST RECIPES

# ALMOND MILK AND FRESH FRUIT PARFAIT

## ALMOND MILK AND FRESH FRUIT PARFAIT

### GENERAL INFO

Serving Size: 1 Cup
Servings Per Recipe: 1
Calories: 293
Cooking Time: About 5 Minutes

### INGREDIENTS

Apples, bananas, and berries—3 lbs., diced
Granola
Almond milk yogurt—as required for the fruits
Nuts

### NUTRITION INFO

Carbohydrate—62 g
Protein—10 g
Fat—2 g
Sodium—268 mg
Cholesterol—5 mg

## ALMOND MILK AND FRESH FRUIT PARFAIT

### DIRECTIONS

1. Make a layer of granola in a glass cup, and then, top it with almond yogurt. Layer nuts and then chopped fruits.
2. Keep following the layering process until you fill your glass cup completely.
3. Put in your refrigerator for about 20–30 minutes.
4. Your dish is ready to be served.

# Recipe Notes

# BANANA ALMOND OATMEAL

## BANANA ALMOND OATMEAL

### GENERAL INFO

Serving Size:1/3rd Of The
Recipe
Servings Per Recipe: 3
Calories: 203
Cooking Time: About 16
Minutes

### INGREDIENTS

Water—3 cups
Steel-cut oats—1 cup
Cinnamon—1tsp.
Bananas—2, sliced
Maple syrup—according to taste
Almonds—½ cup, sliced

### NUTRITION INFO

Carbohydrate—34 g
Protein—7 g
Fat—6 g
Sodium—64 mg
Cholesterol—1 mg

## BANANA ALMOND OATMEAL

### DIRECTIONS

1. Take out your Instant Pot and put oats, 1 sliced banana, water, and cinnamon in it. Give a few seconds of stirring.
2. Close the top lid and seal to cook for about 3–4 minutes.
3. The pressure buildup will take about 12–15 minutes. Then, the cooking will begin.
4. Utilize natural release of pressure for about 8–10 minutes, and then, open the lid.
5. Take out the cooked oatmeal and mix another sliced banana, maple syrup, and the slices of almond.
6. Serve and enjoy.

# Recipe Notes

# BREAKFAST BROWN RICE WITH APPLE AND RAISIN

# BROWN RICE WITH APPLE AND RAISIN

## GENERAL INFO

Serving Size: ½ Of The Recipe
Servings Per Recipe: 2
Calories: 231
Cooking Time: About 22 Minutes

## INGREDIENTS

Water—1 cup
Cooked brown rice—2 cups
Cinnamon—1 tbsp.
Almond milk or any plant-based milk—2 cups
Apple—1, chopped
Maple syrup—¼ cup
Raisins—¼ cup

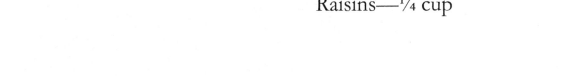

## NUTRITION INFO

Carbohydrate—43 g
Protein—7 g
Fat—6 g
Sodium—298 mg
Cholesterol—7 mg

## BROWN RICE WITH APPLE AND RAISIN

## DIRECTIONS

1. In a large enough skillet, put cooked rice with cinnamon and water.
2. Give about 4 minutes of stir cooking, and then, include plant-based milk as well as raisins and apples.
3. Cook for about 12–15 minutes.
4. Take out and allow the mixture to set for 3–5 minutes.
5. Add more almond milk when serving.

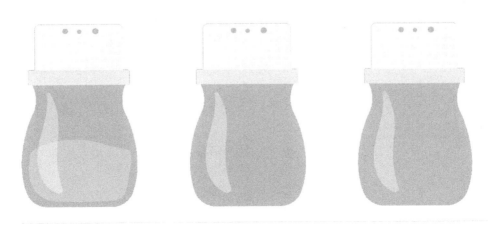

# Recipe Notes

# FRIED VEGETABLE AND POTATO BOWL

## FRIED VEGETABLE AND POTATO BOWL

### GENERAL INFO

Serving Size: 1 Bowl
Servings Per Recipe: 1
Calories: 172
Cooking Time: About 12
Minutes

### INGREDIENTS

Carrot—1, cut into slices
Onion—1/2, finely chopped
Bell pepper—½, large slices
Cooked potatoes—1 cup,
chopped
Jalapeno—1, finely sliced
Leftover beans—½ cup
Broccoli

### NUTRITION INFO

Carbohydrate—29 g
Protein—2 g
Fat—6 g
Sodium—620 mg
Cholesterol—0 mg

## FRIED VEGETABLE AND POTATO BOWL

## DIRECTIONS

1. Take a large enough skillet and heat it, keeping the heat to medium.
2. Stir mix carrot slices and onion and cook for about 2–3 minutes.
3. After that, you can put bell pepper slices and keep stir cooking. Put some water if required. Also, put potatoes, jalapeno, and beans.
4. After heating this mixture thoroughly, you can include broccoli florets.
5. Give about 3–5 minutes of stir-frying, and then, take out.
6. Enjoy.

# Recipe Notes

# MIX-VEG QUINOA BEANS TACOS

# MIX-VEG QUINOA BEANS TACOS

## GENERAL INFO

Serving Size: 2 Tacos
Servings Per Recipe: 1
Calories: 263
Cooking Time: About 12
Minutes

## INGREDIENTS

Bell pepper—1/2, diced
Onion—1/2, diced
Mushrooms—1 handful,
chopped
Jalapeno—½, seeds removed
Baked potato—1, diced
Cauliflower—1 cup, sliced
Cooked quinoa—½ cup
Cooked beans—½ cup, drained
Pepper, salt, turmeric, and
garlic—according to your taste
Nutritional yeast—1 tbsp.
Tortillas—2

## NUTRITION INFO

Carbohydrate—17 g
Protein—3 g
Fat—22 g
Sodium—15 mg
Cholesterol—0mg

## MIX-VEG QUINOA BEANS TACOS

## DIRECTIONS

1. In a large enough skillet, you can cook peppers, onions, and mushrooms, keeping the heat to medium. Stir from time to time, and then, include some water to avoid stickiness in veggies.
2. After getting soft veggies, you can stir mix quinoa, potatoes, and beans as well.
3. Mix thoroughly and include all the spices and nutritional yeast.
4. Take out and equally divide among the two tortillas.
5. Your dish is ready to be served.

# Recipe Notes

# MUSHROOM PEPPER SORGHUM MUFFINS

MUSHROOM PEPPER SORGHUM MUFFINS

## GENERAL INFO

Serving Size:¼Th Of The Recipe
Servings Per Recipe: 4
Calories: 190
Cooking Time: About 25 Minutes

## INGREDIENTS

Sorghum flour—½ cup, whole grain
Flour of brown rice—1 cup, whole grain
Xanthangum—1 tsp.
Tapioca flour—½ cup, whole grain
Salt—1tsp.
Nutritional yeast—¼ cup
Garlic powder—1tsp.
Onions powder—1tsp.
Baked potato—1 cup, diced
Black pepper—½ tsp.
Bell pepper—¼ cup, diced
Onion—¼ cup, diced
Mushrooms—½ cup, diced
Rice milk—1 cup and more
Jalapeno—¼ cup, diced

## NUTRITION INFO

Carbohydrate—29 g
Protein—6 g
Fat—7 g
Sodium—117 mg
Cholesterol—16 mg

## MUSHROOM PEPPER SORGHUM MUFFINS

### DIRECTIONS

1. Prepare your oven by preheating it to a temperature of 350°F.
2. Use cooking spray to grease the muffin pan.
3. Take a large enough bowl to combine together all the dry items given in the ingredients. Also, mix vegetables, and then, include your rice milk. Include more rice milk if you feel to make a consistent texture for muffin baking.
4. Scoop and transfer the prepared batter to your muffin pan.
5. Give about 23–25 minutes of baking. Check the readiness with a toothpick. If ready, the toothpick collects no mixture on the way out of the muffin.
6. Take out and give about 5–10 minutes before serving.

# Recipe Notes

# OIL-FREE PEPPER AND POTATO

# OIL-FREE PEPPER AND POTATO

## GENERAL INFO

Serving Size:1/3rdof The Recipe
Servings Per Recipe: 3
Calories: 183
Cooking Time: About 24 Minutes

## INGREDIENTS

Garlic—3 cloves, minced
Diced onion—1 cup
Bell pepper—1, diced
Potatoes—2 lbs., cut into bite size pieces
Jalapeno—1, seeds removed, sliced
Pepper and salt—according to taste
Water—1 cup

## NUTRITION INFO

Carbohydrate—14 g
Protein—8 g
Fat—11 g
Sodium—209 mg
Cholesterol—192 mg

# OIL-FREE PEPPER AND POTATO

## DIRECTIONS

1. Keeping the heat to medium, allow a large enough skillet to heat up.
2. Include garlic and onion and stir cook for a few seconds. After getting an aroma, include a few tablespoons of water. Stir properly, and then, let it cook on its own.
3. During this time, you can prepare your potatoes and put them in the skillet along with more water.
4. Cover the skillet with top lid and give about 8–10 minutes of cooking. Keep checking for stickiness and include more water if required.
5. Put jalapeno slices and bell pepper to cook for another 8–10 minutes with the lid closed.
6. Check the readiness of the potatoes with your fork and take out.
7. Allow the vegetables to cool down for about 3–5 minutes and then serve.

# Recipe Notes

# PEACH CHIA OATMEAL

## PEACH CHIA OATMEAL

### GENERAL INFO

Serving Size: 1 Bowl
Servings Per Recipe: 1
Calories: 129
Cooking Time: About 12
Minutes

### INGREDIENTS

Peaches—2, sliced
Rolled oats—1 cup
Cinnamon
Maple syrup
Chia seeds

### NUTRITION INFO

Carbohydrate—23 g
Protein—3 g
Fat—3 g
Sodium—9 mg
Cholesterol—6 mg

## PEACH CHIA OATMEAL

### DIRECTIONS

1. Slice the peaches and peel them as well.
2. Heat a small-sized saucepan on medium heat. Put peaches with a little quantity of water to give about 3–4 minutes of cooking.
3. Transfer half of the peach mixture to your food processor or blender to make a puree. Keep the rest of the slices aside.
4. Cook oats and mix peach puree and slices.
5. Stir mix and heat thoroughly.
6. Take out and top with maple syrup, chia seeds, and cinnamon.
7. Enjoy!

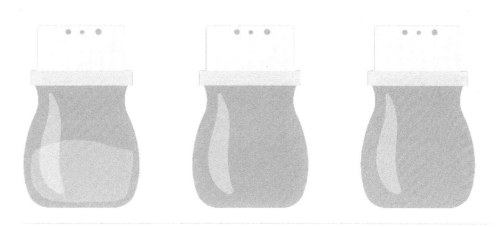

# Recipe Notes

# POMEGRANATE NUTS QUINOA

## POMEGRANATE NUTS QUINOA

### GENERAL INFO

Serving Size: 1 Bowl
Servings Per Recipe: 1
Calories: 154
Cooking Time: About 5 Minutes

### INGREDIENTS

Cooked quinoa—1 cup
Nuts—as per your need
Fresh pomegranate—as per your need
Almond milk—as per your need
Cinnamon—as per your need

### NUTRITION INFO

Carbohydrate—21 g
Protein—5 g
Fat—6 g
Sodium—440 mg
Cholesterol—0 mg

## POMEGRANATE NUTS QUINOA

### DIRECTIONS

1. Take a small pan and put it on the heating platform.
2. Include cooked quinoa to heat thoroughly, and then, include almond milk and cinnamon.
3. Mix properly, and then, take out.
4. Top it with pomegranate and serve.

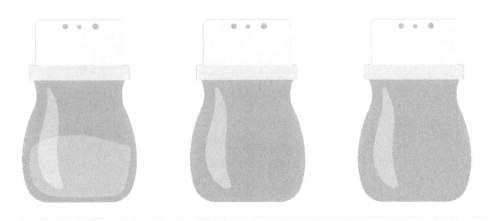

# Recipe Notes

# STEVIE BERRY QUINOA BOWL FOR BREAKFAST

## STEVIE BERRY QUINOA BOWL

### GENERAL INFO

Serving Size: 1 Bowl
Servings Per Recipe: 1
Calories: 233
Cooking Time: About 5 Minutes

### INGREDIENTS

Vanilla—¼tsp.
Cooked quinoa—1 cup
Mix berries—½ cup,
strawberries, raspberries, and
blueberries
Rice milk—2 tbsps.
Chia seeds—as required for the
mixture

### NUTRITION INFO

Carbohydrate—42 g
Protein—6 g
Fat—6 g
Sodium—5 mg
Cholesterol—0 mg

## STEVIE BERRY QUINOA BOWL

### DIRECTIONS

1. Use cold or warm quinoa to mix with rice milk, vanilla, chia seed, and berries.
2. Enjoy.

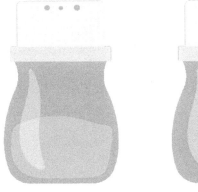

# Recipe Notes

# STRAWBERRY BANANA BOWL OF SMOOTHIE

## STRAWBERRY BANANA BOWL OF SMOOTHIE

### GENERAL INFO

Serving Size: 1 Bowl
Servings Per Recipe: 1
Calories: 250
Cooking Time: About 8 Minutes

### INGREDIENTS

Banana—2
Plant-based milk—4 ounces
Fresh strawberries—12
Fresh blueberries—½ cup

### NUTRITION INFO

Carbohydrate—64 g
Protein—3 g
Fat—5 g
Sodium—12 mg
Cholesterol—10 mg

## STRAWBERRY BANANA BOWL OF SMOOTHIE

### DIRECTIONS

1. In your blender, put the available plant-originated milk along with 1 sliced banana and half of the strawberries.
2. Blend to make a smoothie-like consistency.
3. In a small-sized bowl, include the smoothie and top it with strawberries, slices of banana, and blueberries as well.
4. Enjoy.

# Recipe Notes

# TANGY FRESH FOOD SALAD

## TANGY FRESH FOOD SALAD

### GENERAL INFO

Serving Size: 1 Glass
Servings Per Recipe: 1
Calories: 137
Cooking Time: About 6 Minutes

### INGREDIENTS

Strawberries—3, chopped, fresh
Blueberries—a handful
Mangoes—½, diced
Kiwi—1, sliced after peeling
Lemon and lime—1 each, juiced
together

### NUTRITION INFO

Carbohydrate—32 g
Protein—3 g
Fat—1 g
Sodium—30 mg
Cholesterol—3 mg

## TANGY FRESH FOOD SALAD

### DIRECTIONS

1. In a glass or bowl, mix all the fruits.
2. Add lime and lemon juice mixture and toss properly.
3. Enjoy.

# Recipe Notes

# VANILLA BANANA STRAWBERRY MUFFINS

## VANILLA BANANA STRAWBERRY MUFFINS

### GENERAL INFO

Serving Size: 1 Muffin
Servings Per Recipe: 12
Calories: 91
Cooking Time: About 30
Minutes

### INGREDIENTS

Sugar—½ cup
Bananas—½ cup
Plant-originated milk—½ cup,
almond, soy, or rice milk
Vanilla—1 tsp.
Salt—¼ tsp.
Baking soda—1 tsp.
Diced strawberries—2 cups,
fresh
All-purpose flour—1 ¾ cups,
whole wheat
Bananas—½ cup, finely diced

### NUTRITION INFO

Carbohydrate—21 g
Protein—3 g
Fat—1 g
Sodium—235 mg
Cholesterol—16 mg

## VANILLA BANANA STRAWBERRY MUFFINS

### DIRECTIONS

1. Prepare your oven by preheating it to a temperature of about 350°F.
2. Line the available muffin pan with parchment liners.
3. Take a large enough bowl to mash and mix 2 of the available bananas, vanilla, sugar, and plant-originated milk. Make a consistent mixture.
4. Include baking soda along with the flour and salt. Blend properly to make a consistent batter.
5. In the prepared mixture, you can fold mix the pieces of strawberries and bananas.
6. Equallydivide this batter to all the holes in your muffin tin.
7. Transfer to the preheated oven to bake for about 27–30 minutes.
8. Check the readiness of the muffins with a toothpick, and then, take out.
9. Give 5 minutes to cool down, and then, serve.

# Recipe Notes

# PLANT BASED SOUPS AND SALADS RECIPES

"One should not kill a living being, nor cause it to be killed, nor should one incite another to kill. Do not injure any being, either strong or weak, in the world."
- Budha

# BROWN RICE AND CHICKPEA SOUP

# BROWN RICE AND CHICKPEA SOUP

## GENERAL INFO

Serving Size:1/6thof The Recipe
Servings Per Recipe: 6
Calories: 394
Cooking Time: About 30
Minutes

## INGREDIENTS

Brown rice—1 cup
Dry chickpeas—1 cup
Sliced carrots—2 cups
Water—4 cups
Chopped celery—2 cups
Diced onion—1 cup
Nutritional yeast—½ cup
Water—4 cups
Onion powder—2tsps.
Salt—2tsps.
Parsley flakes—1 tsp.
Garlic powder—2tsps.
Paprika—½ tsp.

## NUTRITION INFO

Carbohydrate—64 g
Protein—13 g
Fat—11 g
Sodium—1,049 mg
Cholesterol—0 mg

## BROWN RICE AND CHICKPEA SOUP

### DIRECTIONS

1. In your soup pot or an Instant Pot, you can put all the rice along with chickpeas. Now, fill this mixture with water.
2. Close the top lid and seal the pot.
3. Give about 25–30 minutes to cooking, keeping the pressure on high.
4. Let the natural release of pressure occur for about 5–10 minutes.
5. Open the top lid and include all the other vegetables, spices, and more water.
6. Stir mix it all and close the top lid again.
7. Cook for 4–5 extra minutes, keeping the pressure on high.
8. Allow for natural release of pressure, and then, open to serve.

# Recipe Notes

# BUTTERNUT SQUASH CRANBERRY SALAD WITH QUINOA

# BUTTERNUT SQUASH CRANBERRY SALAD WITH QUINOA

## GENERAL INFO

Serving Size: 1 Bowl
Servings Per Recipe: 1
Calories: 266
Cooking Time: About 10
Minutes

## INGREDIENTS

Cooked quinoa—1 cup
Salad greens—3 cups
Ginger—1 tsp., grated freshly
Butternut squash—½ cup,
steamed
Onion—¼, chopped
Cranberries—2 tbsps.

## NUTRITION INFO

Carbohydrate—32 g
Protein—8 g
Fat—16 g
Sodium—41 mg
Cholesterol—4 mg

# BUTTERNUT SQUASH CRANBERRY SALAD WITH QUINOA

## DIRECTIONS

1. In a heated skillet, you can add onions and let it get a little crispy by stir cooking.
2. Take a large enough bowl to make a mixture of squash, cranberries, and quinoa. Also, stir mix ginger.
3. Plate over fresh greens along with the crispy onions.
4. Enjoy.

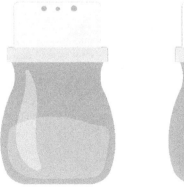

# Recipe Notes

# CHICKPEA PEPPER SALAD WITH BBQ SAUCE

## CHICKPEA PEPPER SALAD WITH BBQ SAUCE

### GENERAL INFO

Serving Size: 1 Bowl
Servings Per Recipe: 1
Calories: 157
Cooking Time: About 5 Minutes

### INGREDIENTS

BBQ sauce—3 tbsps.
Cooked chickpeas—1 cup
Tomatoes—2, small, diced
Leafy greens—a handful, chopped
Carrots—2, small, diced
Peppers—½, diced
Onions—2, small, chopped
Mushrooms and cucumbers—optional

### NUTRITION INFO

Carbohydrate—19 g
Protein—4 g
Fat—8 g
Sodium—224 mg
Cholesterol—0 mg

## CHICKPEA PEPPER SALAD WITH BBQ SAUCE

### DIRECTIONS

1. Take a large enough pan to properly heat the cooked chickpeas.
2. Include the BBQ sauce and stir mix properly. Reduce the heat and cook on low for 2 minutes.
3. Switch off the heat and include all the chopped vegetables. Enjoy

# Recipe Notes

# CORN BEANS AVOCADO SALAD

## CORN BEANS AVOCADO SALAD

## GENERAL INFO

Serving Size: 1 Bowl
Servings Per Recipe: 1
Calories: 184
Cooking Time: About 5 Minutes

## INGREDIENTS

Cooked black beans—1 cup
Cooked grain of your choice—choose whole grain
Lettuce—chopped
Avocado—1, sliced
Cooked corn—enough for the beans, organic
Lime juice

## NUTRITION INFO

Carbohydrate—27 g
Protein—8 g
Fat—7 g
Sodium—79 mg
Cholesterol—0 mg

## CORN BEANS AVOCADO SALAD

## DIRECTIONS

1. Take a large enough bowl to mix all the given ingredients.
2. Toss properly and serve.

# Recipe Notes

# GARLIC BROCCOLI AND POTATO SOUP

## GARLIC BROCCOLI AND POTATO SOUP

### GENERAL INFO

Serving Size:1/6thof The Recipe
Servings Per Recipe: 6
Calories: 149
Cooking Time: About 22
Minutes

### NUTRITION INFO

Carbohydrate—28 g
Protein—5 g
Fat—2 g
Sodium—326 mg
Cholesterol—1 mg

### INGREDIENTS

Onion—½, diced
Potatoes—2 lbs.
Celery—1 stick, sliced
Water—as required for potatoes
Bay leaf—1
Carrot—1, sliced
Pepper and salt—according to
taste
Broccoli—1 crown, chopped
Nutritional yeast—1 tbsp.
Garlic powder—½ tsp.
Plant milk of your choice—¼
cup

# GARLIC BROCCOLI AND POTATO SOUP

## DIRECTIONS

1. Wash, peel, and cut the potatoes into tiny pieces. Put these pieces in a large enough pot along with water to cover.
2. Boil this pot, keeping the temperature on medium. Include carrot and onion pieces along with the bay leaf.
3. Bring it to boil and ensure tenderness of potatoes and carrot pieces.
4. Now, you can include broccoli and put all the spices as well.
5. Give about 6–9 minutes of simmering.
6. Include plant milk along with nutritional yeast and mix properly to get a smooth texture.
7. Your dish is ready to be served.

# Recipe Notes

# GARLIC SMOOTH TOMATO SOUP

## GARLIC SMOOTH TOMATO SOUP

### GENERAL INFO

Serving Size:¼Th Of The Recipe
Servings Per Recipe: 4
Calories: 99
Cooking Time: About 22 Minutes

### INGREDIENTS

Large onion—1, chopped
Tomatoes—9
Celery—3 ribs, chopped
Carrots—3, chopped
Garlic—8 cloves
Water—2 cups

### NUTRITION INFO

Carbohydrate—14 g
Protein—3 g
Fat—4 g
Sodium—212 mg
Cholesterol—0 mg

# GARLIC SMOOTH TOMATO SOUP

## DIRECTIONS

1. In your instant cooking pot or a stock pot, include garlic and onions and give about 2 minutes of stir cooking. Put a little amount of water to avoid stickiness.
2. Then, include all the vegetables and close the top lid.
3. Give about 18–20 minutes of cooking, keeping the pressure on high.
4. Carefully release all the internal pressure, before opening the pot.
5. Transfer the mixture to your food processor or a blender. Blend to get the desired consistency. Adjust salt and serve.

# Recipe Notes

# LENTIL POTATO VEGETABLE SOUP

## LENTIL POTATO VEGETABLE SOUP

### GENERAL INFO

Serving Size:1/6thof The Recipe
Servings Per Recipe: 6
Calories: 229
Cooking Time: About 30
Minutes

### INGREDIENTS

Potatoes—6, diced
Diced onions—1 cup
Chopped broccoli—3 cups
Large carrots—3, sliced
Water—2 quarts
Dry lentils—1 cup
Black pepper—½ tsp.
Salt—1tsp.
Onion powder—1tsp.
Paprika—½ tsp.
Bay leaf—1
Thyme—½tsp.

### NUTRITION INFO

Carbohydrate—31 g
Protein—8 g
Fat—9 g
Sodium—1,082 mg
Cholesterol—0 mg

## LENTIL POTATO VEGETABLE SOUP

### DIRECTIONS

1. Take a large enough pot to include all the vegetables and heat them, keeping the temperature on medium.
2. Include lentils along with water. Put the available spices before closing the top lid of the pot.
3. Give about 25–30 minutes of simmering.
4. Check the readiness of the vegetables.
5. Get rid of the bay leaf and enjoy.

# Recipe Notes

# MANGO BEAN SALAD

## MANGO BEAN SALAD

### GENERAL INFO

Serving Size: 1 Bowl
Servings Per Recipe: 1
Calories: 332
Cooking Time: About 10
Minutes

### INGREDIENTS

Black beans—½ cup, drained and rinsed
Romaine lettuce—3 cups, roughly chopped
Diced tomato—1.5 cups, no seeds
Organic corn—½ cup
Mango—¼, diced
Diced onion—¼ cup
Jalapeno—according to taste, diced
Lime—1, juiced

### NUTRITION INFO

Carbohydrate—40 g
Protein—13 g
Fat—15 g
Sodium—225 mg
Cholesterol—0 mg

## MANGO BEAN SALAD

### DIRECTIONS

1. Take a large enough bowl to layer lettuce slices and put beans, tomatoes, corn, onion, and chopped mango pieces on it.
2. Adjust the spices and stir properly.
3. Pour the juice of lime and stir mix properly.
4. Your dish is ready to be served.

# Recipe Notes

# QUINOA VEGGIES WITH LENTILS

# QUINOA VEGGIES WITH LENTILS

## GENERAL INFO

Serving Size: 1 Bowl
Servings Per Recipe: 1
Calories: 242
Cooking Time: About 5 Minutes

## INGREDIENTS

Cooked quinoa—½ cup
Cooked lentils—½ cup
Cucumbers—¼ cup, chopped
Diced tomatoes—¼ cup
Red onions—1/8 cup, chopped
Mixed greens—3 cups

## NUTRITION INFO

Carbohydrate—22 g
Protein—5 g
Fat—15 g
Sodium—37 mg
Cholesterol—0 mg

## QUINOA VEGGIES WITH LENTILS

## DIRECTIONS

1. Take a small-sized pan to heat through quinoa and lentils together.
2. Take out and include greens along with veggies.
3. Toss properly and enjoy.

# Recipe Notes

# TANGY CUCUMBER PASTA SALAD

## TANGY CUCUMBER PASTA SALAD

### GENERAL INFO

Serving Size: 1 Bowl
Servings Per Recipe: 3
Calories: 268
Cooking Time: About 10
Minutes

### INGREDIENTS

Cherry tomatoes—1 cup, halved
Pasta—8 oz., wholegrain, gluten-free
Red onion—¼ cup, diced
Diced cucumber—½ cup
Lemon—1, juiced
Lime—1, small, juiced

### NUTRITION INFO

Carbohydrate—46 g
Protein—14 g
Fat—3 g
Sodium—546 mg
Cholesterol—3 mg

# TANGY CUCUMBER PASTA SALAD

## DIRECTIONS

1. Prepare your pasta according to your general method or according to the instructions given in the package.
2. Take a small-sized bowl to make a mixture of all the vegetables and mix lime and lemon juices.
3. After cooking, drain the pasta and let it go through the cold water once.
4. Transfer pasta to the veggie mixture after draining.
5. Let the mixture refrigerate for a while or serve immediately.

# Recipe Notes

# VEGGIES AND NOODLE SOUP

# VEGGIES AND NOODLE SOUP

## GENERAL INFO

Serving Size:1/3rdof The Recipe
Servings Per Recipe: 3
Calories: 161
Cooking Time: About 18
Minutes

## INGREDIENTS

Carrot—1, chopped
Diced onion—½
Water—4 cups
Celery—2, chopped
Cooked chickpeas—1 ½ cups
Vegetable broth—3 tbsps.
Dried parsley—2tsps.
Noodles—1 cup, whole grain
Pepper and salt—according to
your taste

## NUTRITION INFO

Carbohydrate—31 g
Protein—7 g
Fat—2 g
Sodium—1,228 mg
Cholesterol—0 mg

## VEGGIES AND NOODLE SOUP

### DIRECTIONS

1. Use a large enough pot to heat all the chopped vegetables along with water. Stir from time to time.
2. After tendering the veggies, you can include the broth as well as the cooked chickpeas.
3. Give about 12–15 minutes of simmering.
4. Include noodles and see if more water is required. Keep cooking for another 12–15 minutes.
5. Put parsley and stir properly.
6. Adjust pepper and salt to taste and serve warm.

# Recipe Notes

# PLANT BASED MEAL RECIPES

*"I hold that the more helpless a creature, the more entitled it is to protection by man from the cruelty of man"*
*- Mohandas Gandhi*

# BEAN AVOCADO VEGETABLE BURRITO

## BEAN AVOCADO VEGETABLE BURRITO

### GENERAL INFO

Serving Size: 1 Burrito
Servings Per Recipe: 1
Calories: 532
Cooking Time: About 12
Minutes

### INGREDIENTS

Lettuce
Tortilla—1, whole grain
Diced tomatoes—1, small
Black beans—1 cup, cooked
Organic corn—cooked
Avocado salsa—as required for
burrito, no added flavors
Guacamole

### NUTRITION INFO

Carbohydrate—58 g
Protein—25 g
Fat—24 g
Sodium—1,114 mg
Cholesterol—196 mg

# BEAN AVOCADO VEGETABLE BURRITO

## DIRECTIONS

1. Take a large enough skillet and heat it, keeping the temperature on medium.
2. Include corn and beans to heat thoroughly.
3. In the tortilla, add the heated mixture and layer all the toppings.
4. Wrap and enjoy.

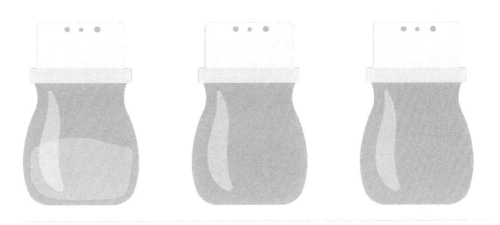

# Recipe Notes

# BEAN ENCHILADAS WITH SPICY RICE MILK SAUCE

# BEAN ENCHILADAS WITH SPICY RICE MILK SAUCE

## GENERAL INFO

Serving Size:¼Th Of The Recipe
Servings Per Recipe: 4
Calories: 425
Cooking Time: About 30 Minutes

## NUTRITION INFO

Carbohydrate—58 g
Protein—23 g
Fat—14 g
Sodium—1,101 mg
Cholesterol—27 mg

## INGREDIENTS

To Cook Enchiladas:
Garlic powder—1tsp.
White beans—4 cups, already cooked
Salt—1tsp.
Onion powder—2tsps.
Corn tortillas—whole grain
To cook the sauce:
Flour of brown rice—4 tbsps.
Nutritional yeast—3 tbsps.
Rice milk—2 cups
Garlic powder—1 ½ tsps.
Onion powder—1 ½ tsps.
Green chilies—2 oz., chopped

## BEAN ENCHILADAS WITH SPICY RICE MILK SAUCE

## DIRECTIONS

1. You can put the cooked beans in your food processor along with the spices to make a puree. Include some water if required.
2. In your baking dish, layer the pieces of tortillas and top it with the bean mixture. Set aside.
3. To prepare the sauce, you can include all spices, flour, and chilies in a small-sized skillet. Give about 2 minutes of toasting, and then, include the rice milk and stir properly.
4. Give about 5–6 minutes of simmering to get a thick consistency.
5. Include nutritional yeasts and stir again.
6. Now, you can pour this sauce over the layer in the baking dish.
7. Prepare your oven by preheating it to a temperature of about 350°F.
8. Bake for about 18–22 minutes.
9. Take out and check the readiness with a toothpick.
10. Your dish is ready to be served.

# Recipe Notes

# BLACK BEAN GARLIC BROWN RICE

# BLACK BEAN GARLIC BROWN RICE

## GENERAL INFO

Serving Size: 1 Bowl
Servings Per Recipe: 4
Calories: 538
Cooking Time: About 30
Minutes

## INGREDIENTS

Green pepper—1 oz.
Cauliflower—1 cup
Tomato—1 oz.
Broccoli—1 cup, chopped
Onion—1 cup, chopped
Water—9 cups
Brown rice—2 cups
Black beans—2 cups
Limes—2, juiced
Salt—1tsp.
Garlic—4 cloves, minced

## NUTRITION INFO

Carbohydrate—87 g
Protein—19 g
Fat—16 g
Sodium—309 mg
Cholesterol—0 mg

# BLACK BEAN GARLIC BROWN RICE

## DIRECTIONS

1. Take out your Instant Pot and put the garlic and diced onion in it.
2. Also, include black beans and brown rice.
3. Put all the water along with the salt.
4. Stir mix all the veggies and close the top lid to seal.
5. Give about 25–26 minutes of cooking.
6. Utilize natural release of pressure for about 10–12 minutes.
7. Open the top lid and stir mix the lime juice.
8. Your dish is ready to be served.

# Recipe Notes

# BROWN NOODLES WITH PEAS AND CARROTS

# BROWN NOODLES WITH PEAS AND CARROTS

## GENERAL INFO

Serving Size: ¼Th of The Recipe
Servings Per Recipe: 4
Calories: 389
Cooking Time: About 12
Minutes

## INGREDIENTS

Carrots—3, sliced
Noodles of brown rice—1
package
Tamari sauce—2 tbsps.
Fresh peas—1 cup

## NUTRITION INFO

Carbohydrate—53 g
Protein—6 g
Fat—17 g
Sodium—707 mg
Cholesterol—0 mg

# BROWN NOODLES WITH PEAS AND CARROTS

## DIRECTIONS

1. Boil enough water in a large enough pot to include sliced carrots.
2. After 2–4 minutes, you can include peas as well as the noodles of brown rice.
3. Give this mixture about 4–6 minutes of cooking.
4. Check the readiness and give more time if required.
5. Remove the excess water and include tamari sauce and stir properly.
6. Your dish is ready to be served.

# Recipe Notes

# BROWN RICE AND LENTILS DINNER

# BROWN RICE AND LENTILS

## GENERAL INFO

Serving Size: 1 Bowl
Servings Per Recipe: 4
Calories: 396
Cooking Time: About 30
Minutes

## INGREDIENTS

Chopped onion—½ cup
Vegetable broth—1 tbsp.
Water—3 ½ cups
Garlic—2 cloves, minced
Brown lentils—1 cup
Brown rice—1 ½ cups
Fresh rosemary—1 sprig
Potato—1 cup, diced after
peeling
Pepper and salt—according to
taste
Thyme—1 tbsp.

## NUTRITION INFO

Carbohydrate—80 g
Protein—18 g
Fat—2 g
Sodium—104 mg
Cholesterol—0 mg

# BROWN RICE AND LENTILS

## DIRECTIONS

1. Take out your Instant Pot and switch on the Sauté mode.
2. Include vegetable broth along with onion pieces. Give this about 3–5 minutes of sautéing.
3. Include garlic and keep cooking for another 3–4 minutes.
4. Now, include water, lentils, brown rice, thyme, potatoes, and rosemary sprig. Stir mix and close the top lid.
5. Seal and cook for about 22–23 minutes.
6. After cooking, allow for natural release of pressure for about 8–12 minutes.
7. Adjust pepper and salt and remove the rosemary sprig.
8. Your dish is ready to be served.

# Recipe Notes

# FRESH BASIL TOMATO BROCCOLI PASTA

# FRESH BASIL TOMATO BROCCOLI PASTA

## GENERAL INFO

Serving Size:¼Thof The Recipe
Servings Per Recipe: 4
Calories: 286
Cooking Time: About 22
Minutes

## INGREDIENTS

Pasta—16 oz., whole grain
Fresh broccoli—10 oz., chopped
Tomatoes—2, large, seeds
removed, chopped
Basil tomato sauce—25 oz.

## NUTRITION INFO

Carbohydrate—40 g
Protein—13 g
Fat—9 g
Sodium—147 mg
Cholesterol—5 mg

## FRESH BASIL TOMATO BROCCOLI PASTA

## DIRECTIONS

1. Take a large enough pot to boil enough water to cook pasta.
2. Put pasta in boiling water and stir properly.
3. Cook pasta for about 4–5 minutes or more depending on the kind of pasta you pick.
4. After cooking that, you can include broccoli and give another 4–5 minutes of cooking.
5. Drain broccoli and pasta properly and include seedless chopped tomatoes as well as the sauce.
6. Transfer this to a large enough skillet and stir heat, keeping the temperature on a low setting. Your dish is ready to be served.

# Recipe Notes

# GRILLED AVOCADO WITH BELL PEPPERS

## GRILLED AVOCADO WITH BELL PEPPERS

### GENERAL INFO

Serving Size: 1 Cup
Servings Per Recipe: 1
Calories: 350
Cooking Time: About 12
Minutes

### INGREDIENTS

Bell peppers—2, strip cut
Avocados—2, sliced
Onions—1 large, strip cut
Corn tortillas

### NUTRITION INFO

Carbohydrate—10 g
Protein—5 g
Fat—23 g
Sodium—178 mg
Cholesterol—18 mg

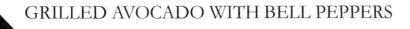

## GRILLED AVOCADO WITH BELL PEPPERS

### DIRECTIONS

1. Prepare your grill by preheating it.
2. Grill bell peppers, avocado slices, and onions trips together.
3. Check after every 2 minutes and grill for about 3–4 minutes on each side.
4. Don't overcook and take out on time.
5. Serve with tortillas.

# Recipe Notes

# LENTIL LUNCH TACOS

## LENTIL LUNCH TACOS

### GENERAL INFO

Serving Size: 2 Tacos
Servings Per Recipe: 4
Calories: 521
Cooking Time: About 17
Minutes

### INGREDIENTS

Garlic powder—according to taste
Chili powder—according to taste
Salt—according to taste
Lentils—2 cups, rinsed
Pepper—according to taste
Tomato sauce—4 oz.
Cumin—according to taste
Lettuce—enough for all tortillas
Tortillas—8
Salsa—no added flavors
Guacamole

### NUTRITION INFO

Carbohydrate—92 g
Protein—22 g
Fat—11 g
Sodium—880 mg
Cholesterol—0 mg

## LENTIL LUNCH TACOS

### DIRECTIONS

1. Take a medium-sized saucepan to cook lentils with enough water.
2. The lentils will take about 14–18 minutes to cook.
3. Get rid of the excess water and make a mixture of all the spices.
4. Mix the sauce of tomato in your spice mixture.
5. Put the tomato mixture in the cooked lentils and mix thoroughly.
6. Arrange equal amounts in tortillas and enjoy.

# Recipe Notes

# MUSHROOM LENTIL PASTA IN ONE POT

# MUSHROOM LENTIL PASTA IN ONE POT

## GENERAL INFO

Serving Size: 1 Plate
Servings Per Recipe: 4
Calories: 578
Cooking Time: About 22
Minutes

## INGREDIENTS

Bell pepper—1, diced
Noodles—16 oz., whole grain
Diced onion—½ cup
Roma tomatoes—2, diced
Cooked lentils—2 cups
Portobello mushrooms—1 cup, diced
Pasta sauce—1 can, no added flavors
Nutritional yeast—¼ cup

## NUTRITION INFO

Carbohydrate—87 g
Protein—25 g
Fat—20 g
Sodium—887 mg
Cholesterol—38 mg

## MUSHROOM LENTIL PASTA IN ONE POT

## DIRECTIONS

1. In your stock pot, you can boil water and include whole grain noodles to cook.
2. During this time, you can get your vegetables ready.
3. Put the chopped vegetables in the boiling water of noodles as well.
4. Close the top lid and give about 15–16 minutes of cooking.
5. Stir mix cooked lentils, nutritional yeast, and pasta sauce.
6. Stop cooking and let the mixture rest for about 5 minutes.
7. Your dish is ready to be served.

# Recipe Notes

# RED BEAN TOMATO QUINOA BURGER

# RED BEAN TOMATO QUINOA BURGER

## GENERAL INFO

Serving Size: 2 Burgers
Servings Per Recipe: 1
Calories: 360
Cooking Time: About 16
Minutes

## INGREDIENTS

Cooked quinoa—1/3 cup
Kidney beans—15 oz., drained
and rinsed
Chili powder—½ tsp.
Onion—1/8 cup, diced
Black pepper—¼ tsp.
Garlic powder—½ tsp.
Tomato sauce—1 tbsp.
Salt—¼ tsp.

## NUTRITION INFO

Carbohydrate—52 g
Protein—15 g
Fat—13 g
Sodium—931 mg
Cholesterol—95 mg

## RED BEAN TOMATO QUINOA BURGER

## DIRECTIONS

1. Prepare your oven by preheating it to a temperature of about 350°F.
2. During this time, you can make a mixture of beans by mashing it in your food processor or your blender.
3. Use the mashed beans and combine it with onions and quinoa in a large enough bowl.
4. Now, you can include all the available spices and mix thoroughly.
5. Pour in the tomato sauce and make a thick and consistent mixture.
6. Divide this mixture into two large patties.
7. Now, you can transfer the patties to your preheated oven and bake for about 12–14 minutes on both sides.
8. Take out and serve on a whole grain bread.
9. You can also add your favorite fresh vegetable toppings such as lettuce, onions, and others.
10. Enjoy

# Recipe Notes

# STIR FRIED MUSHROOMS AND BROCCOLI

# STIR FRIED MUSHROOMS AND BROCCOLI

## GENERAL INFO

Serving Size:¼Th Of The Recipe
Servings Per Recipe: 4
Calories: 358
Cooking Time: About 18 Minutes

## INGREDIENTS

Carrots—2, sliced
Broccoli—1 crown, chopped
Onion—½, diced
Mushrooms—8 oz., sliced
Soy sauce
Brown rice—4 cups, cooked

## NUTRITION INFO

Carbohydrate—35 g
Protein—14 g
Fat—18 g
Sodium—260 mg
Cholesterol—35 mg

# STIR FRIED MUSHROOMS AND BROCCOLI

## DIRECTIONS

1. Allow a large enough skillet to heat, keeping the temperature on medium.
2. Put onions and carrots to cook. Cover the top lid but open after every 1 minute to stir. You can add 2–3 tbsps. of water to avoid stickiness of the vegetables.
3. After getting tenderness in veggies, you can include mushrooms. Now, give about 3–5 minutes of stir cooking. Then, include chopped broccoli and cover the top lid again.
4. Stir cook for 3–4 minutes. Include more water if required.
5. Plate cooked rice with soy sauce and the mixture of cooked mushroom mixture.

# Recipe Notes

# THAI-STYLE CABBAGE NOODLES

# THAI-STYLE CABBAGE NOODLES

## GENERAL INFO

Serving Size: 1 Plate
Servings Per Recipe: 4
Calories: 318
Cooking Time: About 14
Minutes

## INGREDIENTS

Your favorite veggies—2 cups
Noodles of brown rice—1
package
Water
Tamari sauce—¼ cup, soy sauce
with no gluten
Shredded cabbage—4 cups
Maple syrup
Water—¼ cup

## NUTRITION INFO

Carbohydrate—48 g
Protein—12 g
Fat—12 g
Sodium—1,322 mg
Cholesterol—0 mg

## THAI-STYLE CABBAGE NOODLES

### DIRECTIONS

1. Take a pot of medium size and put water in it.
2. Allow the water-filled pot to heat to boil the water.
3. During this time, you can toast your favorite veggies in a large enough skillet.
4. Include noodles in the pot of boiling water and give about 4–6 minutes of cooking.
5. During this time, you can make a mixture of maple syrup and tamari sauce. Include a little bit of water if required.
6. Remove noodles from the pot and get rid of the excess water.
7. Transfer the noodles to the veggies and stir mix the sauce mixture.
8. Your dish is ready to be served.

# Recipe Notes

# WHOLE GRAIN VEGETABLE PASTA

# WHOLE GRAIN VEGETABLE PASTA

## GENERAL INFO

Serving Size: 1 Plate
Servings Per Recipe: 4
Calories: 443
Cooking Time: About 22
Minutes

## INGREDIENTS

Cooked noodles—4 cups, whole grain
Steamed kale—chopped
Eggplant—roasted after peeling and chopping
Bell pepper—1, steamed and chopped
Broccoli—1 crown, steamed and chopped
Onion powder—1 dash
Garlic powder—1 dash
Pasta sauce—1 can, no added flavors

## NUTRITION INFO

Carbohydrate—9 g
Protein—13 g
Fat—8 g
Sodium—1,006 mg
Cholesterol—0 mg

WHOLE GRAIN VEGETABLE PASTA

## DIRECTIONS

1. Take a large enough baking dish.
2. One by one, layer all the ingredients and pour all the spices.
3. Preheat your oven to a temperature of about 365°F.
4. Transfer the baking dish to the preheated oven and give about 18–20 minutes of cooking.
5. Your dish is ready to be served.

# Recipe Notes

# THANK YOU

Made in the USA
Columbia, SC
05 March 2019